He Sent Me An Angel

Kay F. Mason

©2021 Kay F. Mason. He Sent Me An Angel. All Rights Reserved.

ISBN: 9780578895529

All rights reserved. No part of this book may be reproduced or transmitted in any form or by any means, mechanical or electronic, including photocopying or recording or by any information storage and retrieval system, or transmitted by email without permission except in the case of brief quotations embodied in critical reviews or articles.

Unless otherwise noted all scripture quotations are from the Holy Bible, New King James Version Copyright © 1982 by Thomas Nelson. Used by permission. All rights reserved. Scripture quotations marked (KJV) The Authorized Version. Rights in the Authorized Version in the United Kingdom are vested in the Crown, Reproduced by permission of the Crown's patentee, Cambridge University Press; Scripture quotations identified (NIV) are from the Holy Bible, New International Version ®. Copyright © 1973, 1978, 1984 by International Bible Society. Used by permission of Zondervan Publishing House. All Rights Reserved; Scripture quotations marked (NLT) are taken from the Holy Bible, New Living Translation, copyright ©1996, 2004, 2015 by Tyndale House Foundation. Used by permission of Tyndale House Publishers, Carol Stream, Illinois 60188. All rights reserved. The Message Scripture quotations marked (MSG) or "The Message" are taken from The Message. Copyright 1993, 1994, 1995, 1996, 2000, 2001, 2002.

Cover design by: Kay F. Mason and Charlie's T-Shirts
Photography by: Jeffrey Holmes Jr.
Formatting by: K&T Graphics
Edited by: Critique Editing Services

Dedication

This book is dedicated to anyone who has gone through or is about to go through any type of experience that will bring you to your knees. Here is a promise: God is waiting for you like He was waiting for me. With Him, you will come forth as pure gold.

This book is also dedicated to my husband, the love of my life, my best friend, Nurney (Kasem), and my children whom I adore, Kristen and Nurney II; they give me strength to thrive. To my mom, an angel and friend, Dolores C. Hyman who fought the fight and survived, to Mary "Brainy" Peace and Leslie "Lump" Mason who both fought the good fight and God decided He would give them rest. These three women gave me courage to survive.

Acknowledgements

I want to thank my sisters and brothers who stood by my side, my dad, my family, Kasem's family, friends, my Timeout Bench Girls, uncles (my ride or die Uncle Dwight), my newfound cousin "Bunch," Ma Sadie, my sister-in-love Faye, who the Lord saw fit to take home on May 1, 2013 (she made sure I had all kinds of treats!), and my church family of Millennium Bible Fellowship. You showed up and showed out for your First Lady. I appreciate and love you all so much. Thank you, Pastor Anthony G. Maclin, for seeing (literally) about and praying over me and thank you, Pastor John K. Jenkins, Jr for your covering and continued guidance. And a special thanks to my mother-in-love, Marie J. Brewer, who I called affectionately, Mrs. B. She ran her race until August 13, 2020. She and her husband, LB lived in D.C. at the time, which would be a resting place for me after treatments sometimes.

A special note to my sister Linda: You face health challenges on a daily basis. God knew your journey then and He continues to walk with you. You once told me that I was the wind beneath your wings, but really, you are the wind. Remember this, a mirror has no power over you and can't love you. You have God's everlasting love, which is all you need, my everlasting love, and all your family's everlasting love.

There are so many people; I can't list them all, but I just want you to know that I praise God for each of you travelling this road with me, for praying for me, and for loving me. For all of you who came to the hospital for my stay there, I thank you very much; unfortunately, I only remember being in triage!

God has blessed me with such gracious and wonderful people in my life, to walk with me and my family through this journey that only He knew about, then prepared a way, with the help of you Angels.

Thank you to Pata Hall, MS, CPT-TruPata Health & Wellness. Pata, is a friend, survivor and personal trainer, who pushed and still pushes me to exercise and maintain a healthy lifestyle. The Washington Cancer Institute at Washington Hospital Center from the staff of the Mammogram Department to the nurses at the Infusion Center, to Linda Fischer, Chaplin (at the time) and to the Anne Arundel Medical Center, The Geaton and JoAnn DeCesaris Cancer Institute and The Rebecca Fortney Breast Center, thank you all.

Preface

"In all thy ways acknowledge Him, and He shall direct thy paths." Proverbs 3:6 KJV

One day I laughed at myself when I realized I was putting a shower cap on my bald head. I cried at the changes I saw in the mirror, and then smiled that God is the constant in my life and was directing this path. He sent me an Angel, who you will meet later in the book, but I will tell you this: she's possessive, she's a story, she's personal, she's a cause, and she's a calling (thanks to my brother Alex). After my encounter with this Angel, I was led to read Job 23:10 (New International Version) which reads, "But He knows the way that I take; when He has tested me, I shall come forth as gold." He also directed me to Isaiah 43:2 (NIV), "When you pass through the waters, I will be with you; and through the rivers, they shall not overflow you. When you walk through the fire, you shall not be burned, nor shall the flame scorch you." He knew I had to drink the cup of breast cancer and He wanted me to know His promise that He would be by my side.

Have you ever wondered if you could make it through the day or even through the night? Pondered who could you call in the early morning hours and then worried that they would not answer? We all have faced or will face challenges like these in this life, but it is how we choose to journey through them that makes the difference. Choosing Christ is what made the difference in my life. I knew I could not and would not have to go it alone.

This is me. I am a Christian. Raised in the Catholic church, in high school joined a youth group of another denomination, then in college joined First Baptist of North Brentwood where I was baptized and started my journey with Christ. Please understand, a saint I was not! As a matter of fact, a saint, I'm still not. I'm just a sinner saved by His amazing grace. I have an anchor in Jesus that I can hold on to. I acknowledge Him and He directs my path. But sometimes I step off the path and again that Amazing Grace! If it had not been for the Lord, and the Angels that He sent my way, I know I could not have made it this far.

I thank God, who is first in my life. He saw all this coming and prepared the way for me. When He called me to preach (July 11, 2002 at 6:20 a.m.), I wrote Him an acceptance letter in my bible. I hid that letter from my pastor (of the great Millennium Bible Fellowship), who happens to be my husband, my family and friends for a little over a year. I preached my initial sermon on January 11, 2004. When He told me to write this book (in 2010 during one of my chemotherapy treatments), unfortunately, I did not do it right away. The fear of failing Him crippled me. He spoke again, and it was time to listen and step out on faith.

Foreword

Words from My Husband, Friend and Pastor

July 3, 1987 on a hot Friday, Kay and I stood before God and several hundred people. I surmise so many showed up because nobody could believe anyone would be crazy enough to marry me. Let alone someone as lovely and seemingly sane as Kay. We made a vow to support and love each other, "For richer or poorer, in sickness and health," and (get this part) for better or worse.

Though we have been tremendously blessed, we are still waiting and believing God for the richer part. Though by the world's standards we aren't rich. And by the world's standards we are far from poor.

Fast forward 22 years to 2009, just before Christmas the phone rang and the person on the other end of the line informed Kay, she had breast cancer. We had been through some sickness. Like most young couples we had suffered miscarriages. We both had undergone in- and out-patient surgical procedures, but for the most part these were manageable. But then we had to face a real challenge, the big "C." I believe in God. My faith in God is whole, it is complete. But that faith was about to be tested.

Like most people I assumed the worst. I was picking out caskets. We had yet to meet with the oncological team at Washington Hospital Center Cancer Institute. Can I pause for a shout out to the wonderful people over at the Institute? They gave Kay and me stellar treatment. Oh yeah, a month later I was informed that I had prostate cancer. Because of my family history the recommended course of treatment was surgery.

Before 1987 I couldn't imagine life with Kay. Then in 2010 I found myself wondering how I was going to live without Kay. Kay and I formed, or better yet forged a partnership based on God's love. Three years into our marriage we started a business. Ten years into our marriage I accepted my first senior pastor assignment at a church 60 miles each way from our home. Not to mention we were blessed with two children. In 2001 we were led by God to step out on faith and inaugurate a new ministry, Millennium Bible Fellowship. During all of this Kay was right by my side. Up to this point we worked together in the business. In one fell swoop all of this was put in jeopardy.

Our children by then were in their first years of college. Our daughter Kristen, by the grace of God, was in D.C. for the semester on an internship. Nurney II was in his freshman year at Towson University. I resolved to do all I could not to burden them unnecessarily.

It turned out Kay had a virulent strain of breast cancer. We had just witnessed this strain take from our midst a beloved friend and member in less than 12 months. On her deathbed, this dear saint made Kay pledge she would look after her daughter. Instead Kay had to tell this daughter she had the same breast cancer her mother had died from.

Those were some dark days. The lowest point for me came when Kay, so nauseated from chemo, was vomiting in the toilet. I was just out of surgery, so I was unable to lift her up. So we sat in the bathroom on the floor until she was able to move.

I think I need to pause here and categorically say we were blessed with so much support. Point of fact, when I told this part of our journey, my next-door neighbor was enraged. He let me know in no uncertain terms how bad I made him feel that I did not call him in our hour of need. Like I said, Kay and I shared our storms together. We welcomed all the help we received. We just did not want to take advantage of people.

Kay's trek through surgery and chemotherapy was not pleasant. As much as I was able, I took her to her treatments. In the early stages that was not difficult as I was doing follow-ups with my oncologist. We made so many friends at the cancer institute that a lot of times we spent more time ministering to people than we spent in the doctors' offices. There was one incident where one of our doctors sent a staffer down to reception to tell the cancer ministers to bring themselves upstairs.

To say I prayed a lot is an understatement. In my prayer time the Holy Spirit took me back to the hot July afternoon and reminded me of the vow I made. Sickness and in health. But the most important or significant part for me at that time was the part of the vows, "for better or worse." God reminded me when things get worse, I am to get better. As Job once said, "Shall we only expect good from God and not evil?"

I wish I could say God told me Kay would be ok during this ordeal. He didn't. He simply told me to stand on faith and walk by my wife's side. Oh, and by the way, I like to think I wrote some of my best sermons in the waiting rooms of the cancer ward.

It was hard to watch Kay suffer and be powerless to alleviate her pain. One of our love languages (we share all five in common) is giving and serving. At one point, Kay lost her appetite. I was taken back to 1988. Kay was carrying Kristen. She was so sick nothing would stay down. I was in the store frantic because the doctor was threatening hospitalization. I was perusing the bread aisle looking for something Kay could eat. To compound the situation Kay was allergic to wheat. God sent an angel in the form of an elderly Jewish sister. She was so attuned, she saw my frustration and asked me what was wrong. When I explained the situation to her, she told me of her experience as a young soon-to-be mother. She told me to try spelt bread. It worked. Kay was able to eat and to this day she bakes with spelt flour.

Fast forward again, this time the Holy Spirit took me back to one of the cancer sessions. In that session the instructor informed us about the loss of appetite that can occur with chemo. Her advice was to find out what general category the patient had a taste for or a specific food. She explained the tongue is mapped into four areas: sweet, sour, salty, and bitter. She said to have the patient think of a food that fits in either of those categories and eat that. Better to eat something the patient could tolerate than to eat nothing at all. Kay had a taste for two foods: sausage cooked with eggs and chicken and rice. As I said earlier, we had plenty of friends and neighbors who were willing to cook for us. But Kay only wanted those two dishes prepared the way I cooked them. Ergo I cooked them until she was able to eat other foods.

Ten years have passed, and Kay is virtually cancer free. Ironically the pain that enabled the doctors to discover the cancer is still not resolved, and the painful side effects from the treatment persist. But Kay embodies the sentiments of Paul in Corinthians where he said, "We are comforted to be comforters." That is what Kay does. She walks alongside others to bring them comfort. I have seen days where she is in so much pain, yet she sits and listens to others as they pour out their pain.

At the age of 55, God led me to complete a five-year doctoral program. As per her usual self, Kay was right there giving me whatever help she could. That I can now claim the title of Dr. Mason is due in no small part to Kay. I know God will never put more on us than we can bear. But to be honest sometimes I ask Him can He give Kay a little less and spare her? I look at this woman of faith, of character, and strength. I cannot imagine what I would do without her. I pray to God I don't have to. I watch her grow more lovely as the years go by. And I am reminded of the vow I took. When things get worse, I am to get better. So as she walks beside others, I will by the grace of God walk with her. To be there when she needs me. She is always there when I need her. I love you, Kay!

Pastor Nurney Kasem Mason

Millennium Bible Fellowship

TABLE OF CONTENTS

Chapter 1: He Still Speaks 1

Chapter 2: This Cup Didn't Pass Me By 7

Chapter 3: Standing, Then Walking Through My Red Sea 17

Chapter 4: A Place of Waiting... the Silent Cries 23

Chapter 5: Thriving Through With a Gracious God 29

Chapter 6: Lessons Learned at the Foot of the Cross 33

Chapter 7: Brainy, My Angel 39

Thoughts From My Siblings 43

Thoughts From My Mom 46

Inspirational Gems From Me to You 47

A Special Invitation 54

My Go Toos 55

About the Author 56

CHAPTER 1

HE STILL SPEAKS

Have you ever heard your name called and you looked around to see who called? Then if someone was in another room, you would ask them if they called you and if they said no, then you would just dismiss the whole thing? Samuel had the same experience in 1 Samuel 3. Samuel heard a voice and went to Eli, the priest, who had been training him. This went on two more times. Eli recognized it was God calling a young Samuel. He told Samuel, "If He calls again, answer and say, 'Speak, Lord, your servant is listening'." Well, once was enough for me, so I thought.

Thus began my journey. He spoke and I had to make a choice to not only listen, but to obey. My path through breast cancer was nowhere near bumpy. Honestly, it was rugged, as was the path for many others of my fellow Breast Cancer Soldiers. However, I have an awesome Commander-in-Chief by the name of Jesus Christ. He promised me His continued love and protection, so how could I not say, Yes, let Your will be done.

The Lord has spoken to me on two separate occasions so far in this life, and I no longer doubt that I am His sheep! The first one was quite funny. I was at my parents' home in my bedroom, just chillin'. I don't remember hearing my name, but I heard His command. He said go to church and speak to Nurney, (my now husband, who I call by his middle name, Kasem). I got up, got in the car and drove to church. Mind you the whole time I was fussing at God and asking Him why, yet I continued in His will. God had a plan for this marriage to happen. And at the time of this publishing, 33 years later, He's still manning this ship. Thank You, Lord!

The second time I heard Him, He called me by name in a soft but firm voice. He needed to get my attention. I'm not a name dropper, but if you ever had the chance to meet Dr. LaSalle D. Leffall, Jr. (he went home to be with the Lord on March 25, 2019) from Howard University, he, to me, was one of the finest physicians I had ever come across. He has set the standard of care for me, and I have come to expect nothing less. He was also very easy on the eyes! He was my doctor, and he removed the second lump I found back in 2000. He was preparing to retire, so in April 2009, I had to find a new doctor who specialized in cystic breasts. I found a doctor, but she didn't attempt to understand my family history and the need for me to have a mammogram that year. She wanted me to wait for the following year. Had I waited for the following year, this book would not have come to pass because I would not be here to write it.

Let me pause for a moment to share a little "breast drama"!

Back in 1980 I went to the doctor who discovered I had a lump in my breast. I was 22 years old and really had no idea of the seriousness of having a lump and then having it removed. I just went with my girlfriend and told my mom later about what happened as if it was no big deal. I also didn't know at that time the same situation would come back to haunt me 20 years later. I forgot to mention that my mom was diagnosed with breast cancer in 1995. I knew this time I had to be serious about the possibility of breast cancer.

HE STILL SPEAKS

I watched my mom, who I had decided years ago that the Lord always hears her, go through the dreads of chemo and radiation. She was quite sick at times, but never complained. She couldn't read her Bible daily, but she had hidden His Word in her heart and drew her comfort from there. Telling her about my 2000 discovery was hard, yet I knew that whatever happened, I could make it because Mommy did.

Back to April 2009. Because of that doctor's lack of concern, I did not return. I heard Him say that I still needed a mammogram. But I dropped the ball, for seven months, to be exact. Then in November I heard Him again. This time the Voice was a bit louder and had some weight behind it. I guess I wasn't moving fast enough because His Voice became extremely loud, urgent and very specific. He said I needed a digital mammogram. I didn't even know what that was, but He said get it. Mind you, I am without a breast specialist, and a referral is needed to get a mammogram. Who knows that God can orchestrate a situation? I do, and now you do too! It was time for me to have my yearly GYN appointment, but how was I going to tell her that I needed a referral for this mammogram because the Lord said so? Well, I did just that. She was saved and understood. Who but God could have put this into motion? She examined me, trusted what He told me and gave me the referral. Thank you, Dr. Michele Klein. You are a path that He directed me to, my first angel.

Praise Break! As I am finally pulling this book together and seeing how God's work is working, I have to pause and sing How Great is our God (by Chris Tomlin, but trust and believe that our son Nurney does Chris proud!). This song reminds me of Genesis 15:1, when God tells Abram that He is Abram's shield and exceedingly great reward. Since I am an heir to Abram and God's child, then He is my great God and reward. And He's yours too! At the end of the song, comes the traditional How Great Thou Art, by Carl Boberg. Yes, sometimes you have to go back and grab an old hymn to puts things in perspective. Look around, Who but a great God could fashion the world like He has done! Better yet, go back to Genesis 1, where He shows us His greatness. Stars in their places, the sun and moon coming and going. He is a great God and He did all this for us. And He's still doing great things. Always remember to give God the praise no matter what you are doing. He deserves it and desires that we give Him glory.

I had the referral, but where do I go? He still speaks, all I needed to do was ask. Jesus said if you ask in His will, He will answer, and He did. I called an old acquaintance of ours and was given a contact at The Breast Imaging Center at Washington Hospital Center. What I love about God is that when He is in control, He will coordinate the entire journey—if we let Him. I called and I was given an appointment for the following week. Notice that everyone was operating on the fact that the Lord told me to do this. I must be truthful and say that I felt like I was on a ship being steered by the ultimate captain of my soul, God Himself. What I did not know was just how choppy the waters were about to become.

I arrived at the center early to meet and thank the woman who God used to make this appointment come to pass. She was a beautiful God-filled woman, an angel. He sent her my way as He started to lay a foundation for my journey with people that knew Him and loved Him. I still have the mammogram, which I affectionately sometimes call "the smash."

HE STILL SPEAKS

After the mammogram, they had me wait. Since I would normally have a sonogram after previous mammograms, this was no surprise to me. As I was waiting, I met a lot of wonderful women sitting there. Several had gone through breast cancer and some were waiting to see if they were going to get a clean bill of health. And bless God, these women were angels, so we laughed and spoke about the Lord. I left to have the sonogram. When the technician walked out of the room, she was gone for several minutes and that's when I realized something might be up. The doctor came in and said I needed to have a biopsy. Because God had already laid the path of the people who would serve me by serving Him, I got in on the following Monday, December 21, 2009 to have the biopsy. Talk about the favor of God!

Did I mention that I am a big chicken when it comes to needles? With the biopsy comes needles, a fact I forgot and was glad that I didn't have weeks to dwell on that. You know the enemy loves to get in our minds to ruin our testimonies. Reciting Philippians 4:13, "I can do all things through Christ who strengthens me," was helpful until I got in the room. There was no anesthesiologist! I asked the doctor if she would be putting me to sleep and she said no, she was just going to numb the area. Really, God? They had music playing, but it wasn't what I needed to hear. (I did suggest that they have music for Christians.) They were all very wonderful and they kept talking to distract me. Darn those needles! I've never had an object left in me on purpose, but they left a small piece of titanium to mark the spot. That's when I understood why the Holy Spirit had been prompting me to get a digital mammogram because He knew that this pilgrimage was going to be a long one. Then we waited for the results.

John Waller wrote a song titled, "While I'm waiting." It's about what to do while waiting on the Lord. A line that stood out to me spoke about serving God. This song challenged me to do more than just sit and worry. What I realized was that serving Him took my mind off of my situation and put the focus on Him. One way I could serve Him was to continue sending the Morning Inspirational text messages. Every time I listened to the song (and I listened often because waiting is not easy), it reminded me that God was still working on my behalf, and to continue to serve, praise and worship Him no matter how I felt. Psalm 62:5-6 states, "My soul, wait silently for God alone, for my expectation is from Him. 6 He only is my rock and my salvation; He is my defense; I shall not be moved."

This song became my anthem for a while. God was speaking to me through this song. The last few lines say: "I will serve You while I'm waiting, I will worship while I'm waiting." It was clear that was what He wanted me to do. He still speaks and it's my job to listen, follow and obey.

CHAPTER 2

THIS CUP DIDN'T PASS ME BY

39 "He went a little farther and fell on His face, and prayed, saying, 'O My Father, if it is possible, let this cup pass from Me; nevertheless, not as I will, but as You will'."

42 "Again, a second time, He went away and prayed, saying, 'O My Father, if this cup cannot pass away from me unless I drink, Your will be done'" (Matthew 26:39, 42).

On December 23, 2009, I got a call, not from God, but from the doctor. Poor thing, he was hesitant to speak with me. Mind you, I had been praying for "this cup" to pass me by. He couldn't get his words together. Seriously! I had to help him tell me I had breast cancer. Merry Christmas. Just when my mind was about to go south, I saw the gold angel that Mrs. Peace gave to me as a gift. Only God knew that it had been strategically placed for me to see it to remind me that I would come forth as pure gold. Mrs. Peace fought breast cancer until the Lord said come on home and rest on May 20, 2009. I knew that He would not have allowed this to happen if He did not have a plan. The one thing I knew was that either way, I would win. If He takes me home, I win and if I stay with His help, I win. Talk about igniting your faith into action!

The journey was about to begin. I didn't know what to do, what doctors to call or more importantly, how to tell my husband, my best friend and the love of my life. I called back to my new connection at the Breast Center. She first encouraged me, then suggested a surgeon and oncologist. Thank the Lord, I got an appointment on December 31, 2009 to see the surgeon.

Side bar: I must admit something. I'm all about getting doctor(s) appointments, prescriptions and surgeries done before the end of the year. Why? you ask. Because deductibles have probably been met! No matter the circumstances, He still wants us to be good stewards.

Because the date of diagnosis was so close to Christmas, Kasem and I decided to tell the kids after Christmas. Kristen (our oldest) and Nurney had come home from their day-after-Christmas shopping. We were all laughing about their adventure. And then I revealed what I thought was the big bombshell about me and breast cancer. I looked at Kristen, my emotional one, and she was calm. I knew in my spirit that she knew, and she knew in her spirit that I had received the call, and it was not good. Then she told me she knew me well enough to know that I wouldn't tell anyone until after Christmas. My dear son was silent and that's a rarity! Kristen had spoken to him about the possibilities. Why did my daughter have a plan of action? She was attending Claflin University in Orangeburg, South Carolina. She was awarded an internship on Capitol Hill for the semester, which coincided with my treatment timeline. God orchestrated this! I don't think even He wanted to see her suffer and worry. My biggest weight was lifted off my shoulders. They were doing better than I expected. But God!

We still had to tell my mom, dad, my siblings, all my in-loves (in-laws means we are bound by paper, in-loves means we are bound by His blood), our church family, and friends about the diagnosis. Our church, Millennium Bible Fellowship (MBF)

THIS CUP DIDN'T PASS ME BY

had a Christmas play on December 27 and I was dancing in it. I'd had the biopsy and was in a bit of pain. I had to thank God for making it a success. We danced to a song called How Deeply I Need You by Shekinah Glory. The song speaks of laying your heart and your all out to God. That's what I had to do. I needed Him like I need His breath to live or like a shadow needs light to exist. I was desperate for Him because only He could hear, heal and comfort me.

These lyrics were my cry to the Lord as I danced.

Who knew how exhausting it would be to tell family and friends? Church was the easiest place to tell everyone at the same time. When I looked into my mother's eyes, I knew I would be alright. (When I preach, I always look to her because she will tell me the truth about my sermon!) My friend Linda was one of the last people I told, only because her mom, Mary Peace had passed earlier that year from breast cancer. That Sunday we had a guest pastor who preached about expectations and said we needed to expect God to do and to be God. That message was for me. I realized I was starting the new year off in a different direction, but it's the path that God had already laid and had provided the provision. I knew He was with me. Happy New Year, welcome 2010.

Surgery (a partial mastectomy) was pending. For me, having a double mastectomy was not going to make the odds of breast cancer not coming back any greater. Make sure you always do your homework to know your odds. We went on with life, trying to get the little things in order. My friend Dena came over and we had a good time laughing about life in general. Actually, she was pouring into my life, reminding me of how God brought my mom through. She also gave me a gentle, yet firm, reminder that if I had to have chemotherapy, she would push me to drink water like she did my mom!

It was January 5, 2010 when my husband dropped the bombshell that he would need to have a prostate biopsy. Our primary care physician, Dr. Norman C. Smith, was concerned that my husband's PSA level had changed from the previous year. Being the absolute thorough doctor that Dr. Smith is, he wanted to check it out.

Really? Okay, Lord, it's no more than we can bear, right? Then I needed to have another mammogram of my right breast, (I guess it was feeling neglected) and a sonogram of my left lymph nodes. Well, three nodes looked suspicious and I needed a biopsy right then. Kasem was not surprised. He said he knew in his heart and was already praying. He was praying and I was crying because I hate needles! I was thinking, you know what, Kay, remember to look on the positive side, see everything with your spiritual eyes, no matter what. It's not easy by any means, yet it's what He requires.

On Sunday morning, I woke up to get ready for church, but I just didn't feel like it (the first of a few meltdowns). I was biopsied out and worried about Kasem and the kids.

"This I recall to my mind, therefore I have hope. It is of the Lord's mercies that we are not consumed ... great is your faithfulness."(Lamentation 3:21–23 KJV)

It was 9:48 a.m. and church would start in 12 minutes. I was still not ready. My thought at that point was that I was not giving in to my feelings or going to let God down because I didn't

THIS CUP DIDN'T PASS ME BY

want to press. I missed praise and worship at church, but I had it on the way! My soul found rest and peace when I walked in. I could see the joy on my husband's face and the smile from my mother's heart as I made my way to sit with Mommy (yes, I still call her Mommy). I told myself to keep my eyes stayed on Jesus and praise Him when I was feeling down because He promised to lift me up. This all was preparation for the upcoming week, which would prove to be challenging.

I had to be at Washington Hospital Center at least three times that week, and we had to get Kristen moved into her Capitol Hill apartment for her internship. For the first visit, I needed an MRI of my left breast. This required some type of injection, and as you know by now, I hate needles. It didn't help that I have small rolling veins. The nurse told me she had to find someone who could get the needle in my vein. She laughed and so did I, but in the back of my mind, I knew they had one shot at this! It took the third tech to locate a vein. Well, I made it through. Thank You, Lord.

The second visit was a meeting with all the doctors in charge of my earthly care. The surgeon, the oncologist, the psychologist, the physical therapist, the social worker and the oncology nurse. My (When I say my, just know that my husband was with me.) appointment was at 12:15 and I didn't leave there until 3:15. A long but informative day during which I was hoping to find out when surgery was going to be scheduled. Joke's on me! Instead I found out that I needed a biopsy on my right breast. Where did that arrow come from? Inside I was angry, but then the comfort of the Holy Spirit came to calm and ease my nerves.

THIS CUP DIDN'T PASS ME BY

It was the doctor and me again. I told her I liked her but was kinda getting tired of meeting her for biopsies. Maybe we should do lunch! There had been three biopsies in a two-week period. I hate needles! She and quite a few other people kept asking had I spoken to the psychologist. I guess they didn't know how much I talk to Jesus. We talk, it's my job to listen and obey. I did tell myself that if I needed to find a therapist, it was OK; they would have to have a relationship with Christ. I knew the way I walked through this would have to honor God and display the trust I say I have in Him. Did I like that? That would be a capital NO! Yet ... nevertheless.

It was the end of the week and the wait continued. Nurney was home from Towson University. Kristen also came home from Capitol Hill that evening. I was grateful that she was close. Later that evening I went into the freezer and there it was! Häagen-Dazs Vanilla Swiss Almond ice cream! That's my go-to when I don't feel well. Nurney brought me my favorite ice cream. Kristen made the best chocolate chip cookies I've ever had. My husband was caring for me, running the business, pastoring MBF and somewhere in the back of his mind, thinking about his biopsy. And Panda, our Shih Tzu, was sleeping! For the moment, all was well in my world.

It was Sunday morning again, and it was raining. I didn't feel like getting dressed and going to church (just another meltdown). I thought that there was going to be a time when I couldn't make it to church—because of chemo treatments, not my feelings—so I needed to get myself together and push my way through. I got to church on time and what an experience. The Holy Spirit was high in church that day. The praise team was singing "God Favored Me" by Hezekiah Walker. The song speaks of people conspiring against you, talking about you and telling lies about you. Sadly, that had happened to me, yes, in the midst of biopsies. It was a soothing reminder that God still favored me, so what can man do to me—nothing. Psalm 56:11 reads, "In God I have put my trust; I will not be afraid. What can man do to me?"

Here are excerpts from my journal (which I didn't write in every day):

1/19/10

I found out today that my right breast is cancer free. Praise God! Now I wait for the call about surgery. I rested well this weekend, so today I feel a lot better. I did start reading the books that the Cancer Institute gave me, but it is way too much information to absorb, and it's giving me a headache! Kasem is spending the night in Baltimore with the Lead Team-Pastors from our church conference. He was going to go and come right back, but I told him it was okay to stay overnight with the pastors. He needed and deserved a break.

1/30/10

It's January 30 and it's snowing like crazy. I know we have at least six inches on the ground. Everybody is home and I'm pretty happy today. Kasem's biopsy has been changed from Monday to Wednesday. Darn! We were hoping to find out his results by Friday! But all in God's time. Kristen leaves for New Orleans on Wednesday as well.

2/9/10

It's Kristen's 21st birthday. She finally came home yesterday. Her plane was delayed from Sunday to Monday coming back from New Orleans. So grateful that she was able to stay with our friends, the Howards, who loved on her through a break-up and my upcoming surgery. We went shopping in the midst of a snowstorm for items that I needed for surgery. It bothered me because I was so concerned about how she was feeling. When I would ask how she was doing, her response was: I'm just glad to be home. What a way to spend a 21st birthday. But I had a surprise for her that I think she forgot about. Her first tennis bracelet, which was my first tennis bracelet from Kasem. I promised it to her when she was 16 years old.

Then our son surprised us by taking us to see the movie, Valentine's Day. I was so excited because he remembered that I wanted to see it before the surgery, and he paid for it! It was a great day. Life is good; thank You, Lord.

2/13/10 Surgery Day

We arrived at Washington Hospital Center at 9:15. I had not really dealt with the thought of cancer too much. Maybe I should have. Oh well, I didn't. First stop, the IV center. Lord, You really provide. I got stuck four times! That wasn't good, but it had to be done. Darn these small rolling veins! We packed up to go and I saw my favorite doctor again. Reality was slowly starting to settle in. As she was inserting the wire for the surgeon to follow, tears fell from my eyes. They talked me through the whole process. Next it was time to get a mammogram. All that pain and we hadn't had surgery yet. Then on to Nuclear Medicine. I wondered what the heck was that going to be about.

As we traveled my husband was moved again. The nurses marveled at how each time he loaded and unloaded his Bible, laptop and iPod, he had time to pray and get other names for his prayer list (one that he faithfully prays over). The Nuclear Medicine tech told me that the four little pricks should feel like a TB test. Wrong. But back up. I went out to the restroom before the test and I spoke to some women in the hallway awaiting the same test. I gave them encouragement, explaining that the tech said this should not hurt and most importantly that God was still in control and we could get through it.

I was on the table getting ready for the test. I asked the tech had he had this done to him, and he said no. Then I thought, how does he know that this will not hurt? He administered the freeze spray to numb the area and then the needle. Okay, that part was bearable, but the insertion of the dye was very painful. Before I knew it, I screamed and cried. That was only the first one! As I started to explain that it felt like bees were having a stinging party, he injected number two. I eventually had to cover my mouth and cry because I didn't want the ladies in the hallway to hear me! Remember, I said that it wasn't going to hurt and that God was in control. I did make sure to tell them that a TB shot it wasn't!

Time to pack up again and go back to the pre-surgery check-in. Surgery was supposed to be at 3 p.m. but it wasn't until 4:45. During the delay we had lots of visitors and much prayer. What a blessing. Then we were off to surgery. It wasn't until I reached the doors of the operating room that every emotion that had been latent came to the surface. By the time I was on the table looking at those lights, the floodgates of tears opened up, and I said, "I have breast cancer." They didn't even tell me when they were giving me anesthesia. I think they just put the drugs into the IV to quickly calm me down. Recovery was the pits. I

THIS CUP DIDN'T PASS ME BY

think I told them what they needed to hear so I could go home. We left the hospital at 3 a.m., I was home by 3:30, sick at 3:45. We all finally made it to the bed at 4 a.m. It was only the grace of God that kept us. And Panda, our dog, continued to sleep.

CHAPTER 3

STANDING, THEN WALKING THROUGH MY RED SEA

"When you pass through the waters, I will be with you; and through the rivers, they shall not overflow you. When you walk through the fire, you shall not be burned, nor shall the flame scorch you." Isaiah 43:2

It was February 23rd, and I had no idea this day would also change our lives, again. I had an appointment with the surgeon at 8:45 a.m. to check the surgery site and Kasem had an appointment with his doctor at 11:45 a.m. to get his test results. We got to the Cancer Institute, and we both signed in to see our doctors and they took me back right away. I just knew for sure that Kasem was in the waiting room, waiting on me. For every appointment here, we had never been separated. I came out and couldn't find him. I walked over to his doctor's section and they had called him in early to give him the results—without me. This whole time we felt confident that he was going to get a clean bill of health. I was walking around with the nurse, trying to find which room he was in, and we couldn't find him. I was a bit anxious at that point. I finally located him, and as I was walking in, all I heard the doctor say was, "it's early." My husband found out that he had prostate cancer without me by his side. And then I thought, I found out my diagnosis without him. Hmm... But we were never alone because we had the Father, the Son and the Holy Spirit with us. My husband's face registered his shock, and his hands moved to his face, then slid down from the abundance of tears that flowed through his fingers. How and why, was all I could think. He looked at me and said he was wondering how he was going to tell me. I was diagnosed on December 23, 2009 and he on February 23, 2010.

We left the Cancer Institute in a daze. Now we had to tell our kids that their dad had prostate cancer, really? God must have known that we had broad shoulders to carry this heavy burden. For that moment, I forgot He said to give all our burdens to Him. It was a quiet ride home from the hospital that day. For me, all I could think of was how was he going to get through his surgery without me, and how was I going to get through chemo without him?

What's going on, Lord? That was a Red Sea moment I was not expecting. The only thing I did know was that God would reveal the pathway and we would move forward by faith and obedience to whatever destiny He had for us.

We got the kids straight. The way God kept us, especially our kids, is a testimony of His grace and mercy. Next, we had to tell the rest of the family about cancer…again.

In all of this writing, did I ever mention that my husband is actually very funny? We stood before our church family to tell them about cancer, one more time. My husband started the conversation with the church like this: "Men, I'm going to tell you how to love your wife. When she gets cancer, you get cancer too! Yes, I have prostate cancer. It was detected early, so it has not spread. I have a good primary physician, Dr. Norman C. Smith, who was concerned that my PSA rose several points in a short amount of time. Men, get yourselves checked."

STANDING, THEN WALKING THROUGH MY RED SEA

My husband's surgery was scheduled after my first treatment of chemo. Everybody was working to make sure that he could get in closer to the beginning of my treatment rather than in the middle. We had been coming to the center so much that we became the Cancer Couple. One of the guards asked us if we needed a mailbox so we could get our mail delivered there! We knew that we had to represent Christ through all of this. I truly believe that God was pleased with how we shared our story, but more importantly how we shared about how good and great our God is.

Your Red Sea moment may not be invasive breast cancer or prostate cancer, but whatever it is, believe that God can part it for you and then He will travel alongside you and before you.

Here's another excerpt from a sermon I preached titled, "Standing At Your Red Sea":

God can drown your enemies in the middle of your Red Sea. There's a miracle in the middle of your Red Sea when you allow God to lead and protect your coming and going. Notice that not one Egyptian survived. Why? Because it wasn't their story to share. Make sure to testify of God's goodness. It's your story to share.

What's your Red Sea? Do you not know that a Red Sea is just a front row seat to experience and witness God's divine plan coming into action? I did not make that up, I read it somewhere.

Again, what's your Red Sea?

Do you feel like the enemy is closing in on you?

Do you feel like there's no way out?

STANDING, THEN WALKING THROUGH MY RED SEA

Do you believe God can part your Red Sea?

You've been praying for your Promised Land, and all you see is this Red Sea.

You're wounded, under attack—sometimes physically, sometimes mentally, sometimes both. You're tired, depressed, overwhelmed, abused, used, in pain, you call out and no one answers.

You start thinking of your own way out.

These pills look good, this bottle of alcohol might get me through, this gun is loaded.

I don't have any options, no break is in sight, no boat is here to sail away.

The billows are rolling, the storm in me is raging, I'm done.

What now, Lord?

And He says, Remember what you have in your hand. It's not the rod like Moses. You've got Me, Jesus, holding your hand. I also left you the Holy Spirit to guide you, comfort and protect you. When you start feeling like all is lost, think about the Israelites and what I did for them.

The Israelites were at a crossroad of faith. They'd seen the Lord deliver them before. But what they didn't see was a pathway because they didn't know about it. All they saw was what was blocking them. But the pathway was there. A pathway no one knew about except God alone.

STANDING, THEN WALKING THROUGH MY RED SEA

Nothing can separate you from God when you trust Him. When God reveals the pathway, move forward by faith and obedience to your appointed destiny.

No matter what is going on, always remember your Red Sea moment is nothing greater than what Jesus did on the cross. Don't get it twisted, you will come upon another Red Sea; it's just life. Trust and believe in God, knowing that it is for your growth and not to drown you. When you accept Him as your Lord and Savior, you have an anchor in Him. He is going to take you through it, in His own time. He planned it long ago. His greatest birth in you will come from this place called the Red Sea. Because when we are finally broken, relying solely on Him, He will get the glory and we will get the peace and the blessings. He wants us to trust His plan and when He finally reveals the pathway, move forward in faith and obedience to your appointed destiny.

CHAPTER 4

A PLACE OF WAITING... THE SILENT CRIES

I wish I could say that this was really nearing the end, but I was only two chemo cocktail infusions in. This, this place of waiting, is where I really did almost let go. Kurt Carr wrote a song titled, "I Almost Let Go." I truly was at the edge of a total breakdown, not realizing that I was close to a breakthrough. Jesus will always be there to snatch us from the brink of falling. He held me close that day. I thank Him for His grace.

This was a day that I felt like I just couldn't go on. I was tired of waiting and crying the silent cry that only God could hear. This was also the day that God would send His angel to check in on me. Earlier that morning, after several days of hugging the toilet, I became frustrated to the point of letting go. Remember, I had promised the Lord that I would walk through this journey showing His grace and mercy. I was tired of hiding how I felt. I was mad. Mad at how I was feeling, mad that I was letting God down on my promise, just mad, mad, mad. I didn't want another treatment, another Neulasta shot, not another nothing. I told God He could just take me to His home, right then. I was in the sitting room of our bedroom, which became my safe haven, and I could hear life just passing me by. As I sat on the floor, crying silently and pounding my fist on the carpet floor, I suddenly heard a sweet, familiar voice; it was my neighbor and friend, Yvette Lewis. God sent her at that very moment of my despair. She sat next to me and I told her I just wanted to die.

A PLACE OF WAITING… THE SILENT CRIES

She held me and gave me permission to let it all out. She comforted me and reminded me of God's provision and protection no matter the storm. We forfeit our peace and bear much pain when we decide to carry our burdens instead of giving them over to the Lord.

Please don't get it twisted, there were more days of darkness to follow, and He would always send me an Angel. But that particular day, I felt His love and comfort, and that day I would praise Him for it and be glad in it.

Another dark day. My husband had surgery for the prostate cancer, so he was downstairs recouping and doing well. Some people had come over and there was laughter in the air … downstairs. In my world upstairs, in my silent struggle, is where I was. It's true, no one knows the thoughts you think except Jesus. Wanting to die instead of wanting to wait on Him to live. Unfortunately, I had a feeling something was seriously wrong with me physically. I know you're wondering how I could tell, especially with going through chemo! Something in my system was off. I texted Marcia, my friend who happens to be an RN, MSN and she suggested I go to the hospital. I went downstairs to tell my husband that I needed to go to the emergency room at Washington Hospital Center because that's where I was getting all my treatments. Unfortunately, he was not going to be able to take me because he was recuperating. Selfishly and silently I asked God: "Why did my husband get sick?" I was scared and I needed him right then. Before I totally fell apart, Kristen and Nurney said they would take me to the hospital.

I only remember getting to the hospital and then being taken to the triage area. The rest of the journey, I must rely on

A PLACE OF WAITING... THE SILENT CRIES

my dear children for what happened. To this day the kids say that when I was back there I kept asking them for some "happy juice" for my pain. I have no idea if that's really true, so I have to believe them. I ended up staying in the hospital for three days.

Side bar: Gotta love my girl Kristen. My husband's hospital stay for his surgery was pre-planned and he stayed in the hospital suites. I couldn't spend the night there because I had already had one chemo cocktail treatment, so my system was compromised. Kevin (my son from another mother because I was too young to have him!) stayed and enjoyed the gourmet meals for breakfast, lunch, and dinner with my husband. On the way to the hospital, I told Kristen, because she's the oldest, that if they kept me, I wanted a room like her dad's. When I woke up from my "happy juice" I was in the suite. Why did my husband come up the next day saying I couldn't stay there 'cause it cost extra money! Really? Not moving, not happening. For those of you who know my husband, y'all know he made sure he was there to eat the gourmet meals! By the way, I would like to take the time to thank all of my visitors because I didn't and still don't know all who came by. I guess it was the "happy juice"!

During this place of waiting, I had to thank God for the joyful parts of the journey. But the frustration came back and it hit me hard. My three-day stay at the hospital was wearing me out. Then the doctors told me that the chemo was too strong for me to handle. They lowered the dosage on at least three of my cocktails and added Prednisone. I still had three more rounds to go and three more Neulasta shots to go. And I hadn't even started radiation or the Herceptin IV (and when that starts it's for almost a year).

A PLACE OF WAITING… THE SILENT CRIES

With all that was going on, you know the enemy is always lurking, trying to find a way to make Christians ineffective and I was no exception. I was already thinking about the things I wouldn't be able to do. With a compromised immune system, I would not be able to volunteer at the elementary school, meet with the Women's Fellowship, or preach for a while. The idea of reducing the dosage amount of the chemo had me doubting everything. The breast cancer was aggressive; would the lower dose still be effective? Then I had to go back to my scripture in Lamentations 3: "21This I recall to my mind, therefore have I hope. 22It is of the LORD'S mercies that we are not consumed, because his compassions fail not. 23They are new every morning: great is thy faithfulness." I also asked myself, Why did I promise God I would make Him proud going through this? Why?

Here come the silent cries, the tears only God sees and hears. I was still tired of and from the chemo and it was time for radiation every day for six, count them, six long weeks. Thank you, Uncle Dwight and Aunt Sondra for always being there. I love you. I learned from them that I had daily challenges of Solitaire on my phone and computer!

I was weak, yet it didn't define me. I realized that I didn't have to pretend to be anything else. Second Corinthians 12:10 tells me that though I am weak, I am strong in Christ and for Christ. Paul thought he needed the thorn removed to do God's will. But God wanted Paul to do His will with the thorn so we all would see the sufficiency of Christ working in Paul. Of course, I thought I'm not Paul, I'm Kay, and everything has changed. I was finished with chemo and radiation and those nasty Neulasta shots. So why all this pain? No one knew the damage the chemotherapy and radiation had done to my body because it was masked by the Prednisone. Is this another thorn, God? Like I said, I'm not—no, I ain't—Paul. I was praying for relief, but none came. The pain meds didn't work. I swear the pills told me, We don't work on side effects. This was only the beginning of the side effects. Would I ever win?

I felt like I was on this leg of the journey by myself, "felt like" being the operative words. I was not, but it felt like it. My husband was doing great after his surgery and the kids were doing fine, my church Millennium Bible Fellowship and our State Farm office had moved on without me. Where do I fit in? Maybe I was trying to put the old me in this new skin I'm in.

I promised God I would walk this journey with grace. What I didn't know was how long the journey would be. More silent cries. I wanted people to see Jesus in me. What I didn't show very often was the weary and lonely side of me. When Jesus was in agony at Gethsemane, He wept. He became flesh to experience what we go through. Remember He asked could the cup (Jesus' suffering and death for our sins) pass Him by? He also said nevertheless but Your will be done. Maybe I should have shared more about the pain, the sadness and loneliness I felt. More silent cries, and I know He hears every one, and He already has a plan laid out for me.

CHAPTER 5

THRIVING THROUGH WITH A GRACIOUS GOD

According to Merriam-Webster's dictionary, thrive means to grow vigorously, flourish, to progress toward or realize a goal in spite of or because of circumstances.

First, I had to know who I was in Christ, deep down in my soul, before thriving through with Him. I reminded myself that I was not some random act, and I had purpose. I have the DNA of God, His Divine Nature Assigned to me and to you, specifically for me and you. He created you and me with what we need to fulfill our God-given purpose in life. Having His DNA means that we really can do all things through Him. But one thing that we must all strive for is to have good health, so we can thrive in this place called life.

When you know Him like that, you can accept who and Whose you are when you look in the mirror. I always thought I had a peanut head, and seeing myself without hair confirmed it! The thing to recall to your mind is that He created you, knows what's going on with you and will still love you when you don't recognize yourself in the mirror because of chemo and radiation. I'm going to make it, we are going to make it because of the God we serve. I just had to remember that I was passing through breast cancer with a gracious God by my side.

I'm grateful to God for carrying me this far.

THRIVING THROUGH WITH A GRACIOUS GOD

This is an excerpt from a sermon I preached February 2006, three years before the diagnosis. Who but God knew that I would one day see and reread this sermon that was for me! It was titled, "Thrive, Not Just Survive."

Psalm 1:1-3 reads, "Blessed is the man who walks not in the council of the ungodly, nor stands in the path of sinners, nor sits in the seat of the scornful; but his delight is in the law of the Lord, and in His law he meditates day and night. He shall be like a tree planted by the rivers of water, that brings forth its fruit in its season, whose leaf also shall not wither; and whatever he does shall prosper."

Psalm 1, according to Nelson Bible Commentary, basically has two ways to respond to God's Word: either embrace it wholeheartedly or reject it outright. Make the choice, but be aware of the consequences. It's time to Thrive not just Survive.

Survive means to remain alive, to continue living or just existing. I survived going to hell by accepting Christ. That's all. Do, just exist, not grow spiritually.

Thrive means to make steady progress, to prosper, and that's more than financially. To grow vigorously, to flourish. We survived going to hell by accepting Jesus Christ, now let's thrive by studying His Word and doing the work that He called us to do.

Jesus started thriving at the age of 12, growing and flourishing by going to the temple and learning about God's law. He sat with the elders and picked their brains. Luke 2 verse 52 says that Jesus grew in wisdom and stature and in favor with

THRIVING THROUGH WITH A GRACIOUS GOD

God and men. He even left us a helper, the Holy Spirit to guide us. Am I going to thrive or just survive?

We need to spend time reading and thinking about what we have read in God's word with the aid of the Holy Spirit. Chew on it until it's digested in your soul. Study His Word continually. Joshua 1:8 says to meditate on it day and night so you may be sure to obey all that is written in it, only then will you succeed.

Psalm 1, verse 1 tells us how to be blessed, verse 2 tells us what it means to delight ourselves in the Lord, and then verse 3, well that's the reward. The Message version of the Bible says it like this: you're a tree replanted in Eden, bearing fresh fruit every month, never dropping a leaf, always in blossom.

Just as a tree soaks up water and bears luscious fruit and green strong leaves, we are also to soak up God's word to produce actions and attitudes that honor Him. Then, whatever we do in God's name will prosper or thrive, and so will we. Because we are rooted and grounded in Christ, when we face desert-like conditions we can trust and believe that we will bear fruit once again.

T   TRUST God through all the seasons of your life. Proverbs 3:5-6: "Trust in the Lord with all thine heart; and lean not unto thine own understanding. In all thy ways acknowledge him, and he shall direct thy paths."

H   HOLD to His hand and promises always. Hebrews 10:23: "Without wavering, let us hold tightly to the hope we say we have, for God can be trusted to keep His promise."

R   RADIANT you'll be when you stay in His presence. Psalm 34:5 (New Living Translation) "Those who look to Him

THRIVING THROUGH WITH A GRACIOUS GOD

for help will be radiant with joy; no shadow of shame will darken their faces."

    I   IMITATE the Lord at all times. Ephesians 5:1–2: "Therefore be imitators of God as dear children. And walk in His love, as Christ also has loved us and given Himself for us, an offering and a sacrifice to God for a sweet-smelling aroma."

    V   VERACITY, be known to always be truthful. 2 Timothy 2:15, "Be diligent to present yourself approved to God, a worker who does not need to be ashamed, rightly dividing the word of truth."

    E   ENDURANCE comes with a reward when you wait on God. James 5:11 (The Message), "What a gift life is to those who stay the course! You've heard, of course, of Job's staying power, and you know how God brought it all together for him at the end. That's because God cares, cares right down to the last detail."

I read this portion of the sermon from time to time to remind myself that I owe it to God to continue thriving because He continues to be gracious, loving and forgiving to me. It's my reasonable service.

CHAPTER 6

LESSONS LEARNED AT THE FOOT OF THE CROSS

In no particular order, these are lessons I've learned along the way through the journey of breast cancer. No regrets, just lessons learned.

Colossians 3:23 reads, "And whatsoever you do, do it heartily, as to the Lord and not unto men." I guess this means the journey through breast cancer too!

My ultimate go-to scripture to help me thrive is found in Isaiah 43:2, "When you pass through the waters, I will be with you; and through the rivers, they shall not overflow you. When you walk through fire, you shall not be burned, nor shall the flame scorch you." It takes having a scripture deep down in your heart to get through some difficult times. The Word of God is just that, His Word. The songs that we sing can comfort us, but only His Word can transform us.

My God, Jehovah Jireh, is my Provider. Finances. We never lacked. It got very tight some months … No pay back from the commercial mortgage broker, family and friends, denial of disability over and over and over and over again, feelings of being a non-contributor to the household finances, yet God showed us Who He was and Who He is—our provider.

Never be afraid to ask God! Here is a funny of how God provides. I love peanut butter. In my early 20s I became allergic to peanut butter and all things seafood. When I was pregnant, I could eat peanut butter and all things seafood (Who wants to be pregnant all the time? Not me!). When I started chemo, I asked the Lord if I could at least eat peanut butter when I got on the other side of this. One day our son was eating a peanut butter and jelly sandwich, and I had this hankering for a bite of his sandwich. He questioned whether I would break out from eating the sandwich, but for some reason I was not afraid. Well guess what, I can only eat JIF peanut butter and I can eat a Payday or a Snickers bar, but that is it. One day I was sharing with my husband the conversation I had with the Lord about eating peanut butter. He looked at me like I was crazy! He said you had His ear and you asked for peanut butter and not for money? We had not met our deductible and my first bill was close to $20,000, so I guess he had a point.

God, my Jehovah Rapha, my Healer for a lifetime. Jeremiah 17:14 says, "Heal me, oh Lord, and I shall be healed, save me, and I shall be saved, for You are my praise." There will be days when you just don't feel like going on. But because He is our healer, He already has a plan laid out for us! We need to understand that healing comes in two ways: on this side of the Jordan or the other side of the Jordan—in Heaven with Him. Like my husband/pastor says, "Either way, we win"!

Make sure that your caregivers are taken care of. They tend to have deep-rooted feelings about the pain that their loved ones are going through. Keep the communication open. Encourage them to stay healthy and seek professional help if they need to because they are important to you and you want them to thrive.

LESSONS LEARNED AT THE FOOT OF THE CROSS

Know that it is OK to have an I'm-mad-about-everything moment. Notice I said a moment. Our bodies can't heal properly with the added stress of being angry at the world. I tend to hold most of my frustration to myself, and that's not healthy at all. My friend (not naming to protect the innocent, LP) gave me this Dammit Doll (dammitdolls.com). When you see this stuffed doll, you will laugh; that's good medicine! I never hit it hard enough to "whack the stuffing out," but the relief I got from slamming it was amazing! And no, I'm not going to hell for using it! Find yourself something that's safe to do to release the stress, then be sure to run it past your doctor.

My family had to learn how to let people help us. We have always extended ourselves, so it was very difficult to accept help. God will dispense angels when needed, just let them do what God has assigned them to do for you.

Beware of the trick(s) of the enemy. Chemo brain is when you feel like you're living in a fog. It was hard to accept that the way I comprehend had changed and short-term memory loss was an issue. I used to read the Bible through every year. It took me years to get back to that. The enemy made me think that I wasn't being faithful because I wasn't reading like I used to. At one point I thought the Lord had stopped speaking to me. But the Holy Spirit had me look at my notes (I had posted notes all over the place.). He was still speaking, but in nuggets, so that I could comprehend and not be overwhelmed. He also reminded me that I was still sending morning text messages about Him!

Don't spend your days consumed with worry. He takes care of every need that you have. There is nothing that comes into your life that He has not permitted, planned or provided for.

LESSONS LEARNED AT THE FOOT OF THE CROSS

In Matthew chapter 6 Jesus tells us not to worry about our lives, what we're gonna eat or drink, these bodies, or what we're gonna put on. He also reminds us that we cannot add anything to this life. The chapter closes by telling us do not worry about tomorrow because tomorrow has its own worries! We have enough for today. And the beautiful thing is this: He knows everything that we stand in need of and sometimes He even blesses us with our wants!

Radiation can sometimes cause severe burns. An older lady shared this tidbit with me while we were sitting waiting to have radiation (She referred to it as being zapped!). She said to put on Aquaphor Healing Ointment right after radiation. Then "when you get home let the breeze do what it needs to do, so let the girls be free." Guess what, I did not get any burns whatsoever. My radiation oncologist was surprised to see that I didn't have any burns or scars. I shared that same tidbit with him and with anybody else that I knew who may need radiation. Always check with your doctor first!

On days when I felt hopeless, just out of sorts, it was good to know that Jesus was always willing to heal my body, my mind, and my heart. He is our strength, a very present help! One of my favorite songs by the Brooklyn Tabernacle Choir is "My Help." I would sing that song because it reminded me to lift up my eyes to God because that is where my help comes from.

You have to change your perspective. Find the joy in everything. Kasem said he didn't have to shave his hair because I was bald, he was already practically bald! He is the same one who told the husbands in our church how to really love their wives like he loves me. He said he got prostate cancer to go along

LESSONS LEARNED AT THE FOOT OF THE CROSS

with my breast cancer. Gotta laugh at that! Speaking of hair, losing my hair was not my top priority getting better was.

Don't get me wrong, when I brushed my hair and a clump of it came out, it was quite disturbing. But thank God for my hair stylist and friend, Yvette Thomas (now Dr. Yvette Thomas, a Certified Hair Loss Practitioner) of SalonTrenz in Springdale, MD (salontrenzhair.com). We prayed, cried, laughed and she shaved the rest of my hair off.

You are not your hair! A song that helped me with my new look was, "Just Fine" by Mary J. Blige. When I would walk past a mirror, I would sing those lyrics. I realized I had to love this person in the mirror no matter what. Why? Because Jesus loves me, and all is well. I'm fine and you will be too.

When you marry, marry because God told you to do it. When He is truly the center of your marriage, you can endure the rough times. When you marry for looks or wealth, you will not be able to sustain your marriage when you lose your hair, lose or gain weight, or when sexual intimacy has to be put on the back burner. I witnessed a few husbands who left their wives because the wives were too sick or their bodies racked with too much pain to have sex. Only He can get you through those times, and He will, if you follow the lead of the Holy Spirit.

Learn that you can't control anything! Not even the fact that people are watching you. With the aid of the Holy Spirit, you can control what they see and/or adjust your attitude. Follow the Holy Spirit and they will see Christ in you. That is always a good view. Isaiah 14:27 reads, "The Lord of Heaven's Armies has spoken—who can change His plans? When His hand is raised, who can stop Him?"

LESSONS LEARNED AT THE FOOT OF THE CROSS

Remember that no matter what happens on any given day, God is your refuge and your strength for that moment. Call on the name of Jesus and His name alone will fill you with His peace.

You are God's masterpiece created in Christ to do good works, which He prepared in advance for you to do (Ephesians 2:10). He has already written your story, so read it, trust it and work it out.

God knows about your pressures and your pain. You thought you could not make it, yet here you are today and so is He, with His continued promises of protection, peace and provision.

I did not come through the fire of breast cancer or the flood of chemo and radiation alone. He was walking with me all along. He loves me, He loves you and He knows just how much we really can bear, and we can bear it because He is with us.

CHAPTER 7

BRAINY, MY ANGEL

Meet my Angel, Brainy! Here is how she came to be.

Mrs. Peace (you met her earlier in the book) was fighting breast cancer herself and decided she would have a luncheon for some of her friends. At that luncheon she gave each of us a gold Angel ornament for the Christmas tree. I found the Angel to be so beautiful that I had it on display in our family room. Only God knew that that Angel would change my life a year later. On December 23, 2009 the phone rang; it was the breast center, and I knew the news was not what I had prayed for. As I was walking to my office, I caught a glimpse of that beautiful gold angel and I told myself that I was going to come forth as pure gold.

The name Brainy was Mrs. Peace's nickname. According to Mr. Peace, Mrs. Peace could always come up with a great idea about something. She was a very smart woman, whom I loved, with the coolest raspiest voice I had ever heard!

BRAINY, MY ANGEL

Only God knew the power of this small gift. First Corinthians 2:9 (NLT) says, "No eye has seen, no ear has heard, and no mind has imagined what God has prepared for those who love Him."

BRAINY, MY ANGEL

A special thank you to Charles Williams of Charlie's T-Shirts, for taking Brainy and bringing her to life for me on 12/18/2015; she was finally copyrighted on 12/02/2016. Praise God!

THOUGHTS FROM MY SIBLINGS

From: Judy Smith

To: Kay F. Mason

Subject: Kay

At first I couldn't breathe. My next thought was that I may lose my friend, my sister. I felt helpless. I didn't or couldn't protect you even though I knew it was out of my hands. I prayed God would guide and see you through. I thought of your immediate family. Then mom and everyone else. I thought of Vi. I went to the office and told the supervisor that there's a medical situation in my family, namely my sister. I will use Family Leave because whenever she needs me, I'll be with her.

Some days I felt lost and depressed. I couldn't express it to anyone and especially not to you. But then you allowed me to come and sit with you. I felt some hope just cheering you on to drink some water, all the while I'm still in prayer for strength. Yours and mine. Taking you to the hospital for your treatments made me feel useful. Listening and talking to the other patients and nurses helped me cope. God was answering my prayers through these women. They cheered one another on and that made me feel cheerful. I looked forward to accompanying you to the next session for my dose of cheerfulness still knowing this is serious. From what I saw, they made you feel cared for and well, even loved. That alone was worth its weight in gold for me to see a light on my sister's face after receiving that love. You weren't alone because God was constantly with you. What a miracle!

THOUGHTS FROM MY SIBLINGS

From: Linda Hyman

To: Kay F. Mason

Subject: You!

I can still see my sister's face the day she announced to the family that a lump was found in her breast. I cannot remember anything else she said. I went home in a fog and cried. I still had vivid recollections of my mom's battle with breast cancer. I didn't worry so much about Kay, I feared what cancer would do to her body. I mean, really, Kay could deep sleep from a baby aspirin.

Later, when I understood how aggressive the cancer was, I cried and felt selfishly alone. I desperately wanted to stay by her side. I wanted to nurture her, hug her, cry with her and be her strength. I felt sad that I wouldn't be able to be with my sister as she has always been with me. I felt an inner anguish, a ripping of my heart so deep that I clutched my shirt to hold my heart together. I could not be with my sister.

I Love You, Kay F. Mason

THOUGHTS FROM MY SIBLINGS

From: Alex Hyman

To: Kay F. Mason

Subject: Testimony

Well here's my take: The moment I found out my immediate thought was she is going to be ok. I knew Kay was a very spiritual person and took her faith seriously. She also had two children to live for: Kristen and Nurney. She also had Mom, Dad and siblings who deeply cared for her. But above all family was her loving husband, Nurney Kasem Mason. Kasem loves my sister. Our family loves Kasem. I've always trusted him to take care of Kay from the time they married on that very hot summer day in July of 1987. Support systems are important to the recovery process. Having a loving husband you can depend on surely gave Kay some comfort. My experience watching Kay go through the rigorous process from diagnosis to chemo to recovery was bearable because Kasem was there for her.

It's easy for the spouse to get lost in this whole process because the assumption is "of course he's there for her." As I reflect now on that period in Kay's life, I realize how threatening that situation was. My thinking "she's going to be ok" probably was my way of placing my fears and concerns with the knowledge that my brother-in-law would make certain my sister was [is] "ok." Nurney Kasem Mason was not only an Angel for Kay, but for me too!

Love ya!

THOUGHTS FROM MY MOM

To: Kay F. Mason

Subject: From Mom about You

Kay, when you were diagnosed with breast cancer I was scared and worried, but only for a short time. You see, I remembered that God brought me through and since He did it for me, He would also do it for you. And He did. God said He would never leave us nor forsake us and He is true to His word. So, we thank Him, praise Him and give Him all the glory.

INSPIRATIONAL GEMS FROM ME TO YOU

"Fear not, for I have redeemed you; I have called you by your name; you are Mine. When you pass through the waters, I will be with you; and through the rivers, they should not overflow you. When you walk through the fire, you should not be burned, nor shall the flame scorch you." (Isaiah 43:1b-2)

Private property! That is what you are to God! His joy, His masterpiece. Nothing or no one can separate or destroy His private property. You are protected by His blood. Because of Who God is, because of what Jesus did and because of what the Holy Spirit does, you can walk in victory. Your joy, hope and peace are in Them.

God doesn't sift you, satan does, but only with God's permission and within God's parameters (Luke 22:31–32). You can make it through when you know and believe in your heart that there is NOTHNG that God does not know about or can't handle. He promised you that you can do all things through Him because He is the One who strengthens you.

No matter what, always choose Christ. Choose to allow Him to

Cleanse you. Free you from guilt and shame.

Hold on to Him, your life depends on Him.

Open up and let Him fill you up, because

Only what we do for Him will last. You are

Special to Him, His finest creation.

Expect great things from a great God.

INSPIRATIONAL GEMS FROM ME TO YOU

To receive and make room for the new, you must let go of the old. God wants to do something new, so make room. His mercies are new every day. He wants to deliver them to you. It would be sad to see them stamped "Return to sender, addressee unknown." Clear the clutter, clear your mind, let go, open up and receive!

When you take a leap of faith, your fear gets left behind and now you are facing the confidence you need to move forward to the place God has already prepared for you. God wants us to fully trust Him even when what He asks seems overwhelmingly hard. He does not ask or task without first making provision. He always has a ram in the bush.

You are standing at your Red Sea. And trust and believe it will not be the last. Do not get weary and do not lose hope. God is parting the sea right now because we've made it to today and He will keep parting it until we make it to the other side. Along the way, take time to thank and praise Him; take time to learn more of Him and what He wants from you; take time to encourage yourself and someone else.

With God, your world isn't falling apart, He's remolding it and it hurts sometimes. He hasn't left you to fend for yourself, He's doing what He does best, which is caring and carrying you through.

Today is full of possibilities because of His promises! You have made it this far by His grace and mercy! No matter what happens today, remember that God is your refuge and your strength for this moment. Go ahead and praise Him now! Stay open, stay available, and stay on the path He has for you. Call on the name of Jesus and His name alone will fill you with His peace.

INSPIRATIONAL GEMS FROM ME TO YOU

When there is pressure doing God's will, know that He's pressing because He sees the diamond that you really are. Do not give up on Him or yourself. Stay focused on the glimmer.

Breast cancer or any type of health issue, can become a heavy burden that we carry. The interesting thing is that we carry them unnecessarily. Jesus said to give them to Him. Matthew 11:28–30 holds a recipe for promised rest. All we need to do is just come to Him with those burdens.

Sometimes God allows us to stay in desert places. That is when we need to transfer our faith to Him. He knows where we are, His waiting room. And guess what? We have everything we need—HIM! While you're in His waiting room, pray and listen more, worship Him more, and ask Him how you can show His love through serving more.

You can't move forward looking back. If you always look back at what you think you lack, you will never see what God has done. The Holy Spirit can change your mindset in the middle of your circumstances. Glance back, recall to your mind how He carried you through, praise Him, look ahead and then press toward what He has in store for you.

When God commands us to do something, distractions will arise. That is a trick of the enemy. Stay the course by remembering that God's promise for provision is attached to His command. Read Mark 4:35–39.

"In my distress, I called upon the Lord, and cried out to my God; He heard my voice from His temple, and my cry entered His ears" (2 Samuel 22:7). God does not miss any of our distress calls. He even hears the silent tears we cry.

INSPIRATIONAL GEMS FROM ME TO YOU

Whatever your Jericho wall is, don't try to knock it down yourself or you will be tired and frustrated. Give it to God, He can move it for you, in His time. You keep walking by faith and obedience. With Him the wall will come down.

Be encouraged today because you are a child of the most high King! Think about Him and thank Him for another day of grace and mercy. Let His love warm and fill your heart.

"Do not be afraid, for I have ransomed you, I have called you by your name; you are Mine" (Isaiah 43:1). God is a very present help! Be available. Be still. Be quiet. Be listening.

Shift your focus from the big and loud Goliaths in your life. Be like David and compare them to God. You know the power of our great God. Anything sized up to Him is puny!

You can't stop the rain from falling or the dark clouds from forming; what you can do is adjust your attitude with the Holy Spirit. Be a showcase for Him and light up right where you are! Jesus said He is the light of the world. When you follow Him, you won't walk in darkness and you will have the light of life (John 8:12).

Sometimes your mind will wander back to lies told about you or things you have already repented for. Snatch back that thought! Focus on the Lord. You are who He says you are!

The way has been made, open your eyes, look up, get God's perspective to live through and beyond your circumstances. He sees what is going on and wants your trust.

INSPIRATIONAL GEMS FROM ME TO YOU

Never feel ashamed or make anyone else feel shame for seeking a therapist. Like Luke, God gifted these doctors. Just find one that knows it and serves Him.

Feeling a bit overwhelmed? Take a deep breath. That breath was provided by the Lord. Think about Him and how He's protected you thus far. Say His name, Jesus; say it again and again until you feel His power and His presence.

Don't just hold on to Jeremiah 29:11, look at the scriptures above to see the work order God gave the Israelites in exile. Be the best for Christ in whatever situation you are in, making sure the place is better because you have been there with Christ. Be all in for Him.

On the way to the cross, Jesus said that in this world we are going to have tribulation, but to be of good cheer because He has overcome the world. He carried our sins. This is the great love He had and still has for us. It was His obedience to His Father and love for us, not the nails that kept Him on the cross. Now He's in heaven with a prepared place just for us.

You might be bent beyond comfort, but you are not broken. Roots grow deep and always search for the water source. When the storms of life hit, and they will, don't get distracted. Keep drinking from His ever flowing and refreshing fountain. Be like the tree in Jeremiah 17:7–8, it is not bothered by the heat or worried by the long months of drought. Their leaves stay green and they never stop producing fruit. Remember Who your Water Source is, always search for Him, then finish the assignment He gave you.

INSPIRATIONAL GEMS FROM ME TO YOU

Fill up and be fueled by the word of God every moment. When you do not, the enemy will come and find you empty and then become a squatter in your life.

Storms can pop up at anytime and anywhere. Our consistent and always present Heavenly Father will calm our anxieties and take us through, safe and secure.

Choose to not let a rainy day make you gloomy. Remember that it is a day that the Lord has made and everything He makes is good. Rejoice! The Son is still on the throne and the sun is coming.

"Therefore, we do not lose heart. Though outwardly we are wasting away, yet inwardly we are being renewed day by day. For our light and momentary troubles are achieving for us an eternal glory that far outweighs them all. So we fix our eyes not on what is seen, but on what is unseen, since what is seen is temporary, but what is unseen is eternal" (2 Corinthians 4:16–18 NIV).

Above the water a duck looks as though it is gliding, but what we can't see is the duck paddling and churning to stay afloat and to move. God created the duck and we are more valuable than the duck, so imagine what God is working on behind the scenes in our lives. He makes pathways we don't know exist. As you move about, know it's because of Him.

Being in God's waiting room isn't easy, but it's doable because He's right there with you. Serve and worship Him while you wait. My prayer for you: Lord, we put our hope in You, our health and shield. Our hearts rejoice in You and we trust Your holy name. Surround us with Your unfailing love as we wait on You alone.

You are going to be OK! God's promise in Isaiah 46:4 (NLT) is, "I will be your God throughout your lifetime—until your hair is white with age. I made you and will care for you. I will carry you along and save you."

"For this is God, our God forever and ever, He will be our guide Even to death" (Psalm 48:14). How comforting it is to know that He is with us always and will even usher us into His loving arms when the time comes. This is our God!

A SPECIAL INVITATION

To anyone who does not have a personal relationship with Jesus Christ, please know that He loves you and is waiting for you. He waited for me. Only He can forgive you, love you unconditionally, prepare a home in Heaven for you and give you peace and joy right where you are. Just say yes to Him right now. You are not alone.

Feel free to contact me at myangelbrainy@gmail.com to let me know that you've made this commitment to be in relationship with Jesus Christ.

MY GO TOOS
THEN AND NOW

My soft cashmere blanket, the Dammit Doll, Haagen Das Vanilla Swiss Almond, my pearls and my Bible.

ABOUT THE AUTHOR

Kay F. Mason is a Christian, married to Nurney K. since 1987 and they have two adult children, Kristen and Nurney II. She is a licensed minister at Millennium Bible Fellowship (MBF) in Capitol Heights, Maryland, where her husband is the pastor. They own and operate a State Farm Insurance Agency. She graduated with a B. A. from University of Maryland. She is a breast cancer survivor and thriver, is an encourager, has mentored many women over the years, volunteers (shout out to Capitol Heights Elementary, MBF's adopted school), loves the Lord and enjoys sharing His Word. This is her first book.

www.ingramcontent.com/pod-product-compliance
Lightning Source LLC
Chambersburg PA
CBHW061510040426
42450CB00008B/1547